every teenager's
little black book
of God's guarantees

by blaine bartel

every teenager's
little black book
of God's guarantees

by blaine bartel

Harrison House
Tulsa, Oklahoma

12 11 10 09   12 11 10 9 8 7

Every Teenager's Little Black Book of God's Guarantees
ISBN 13: 978-1-57794-625-0
ISBN 10: 1-57794-625-1
Copyright © 2004 by Blaine Bartel
P.O. Box 691923
Tulsa, Oklahoma 74179

Published by Harrison House, Inc.
P.O. Box 35035
Tulsa, Oklahoma 74153

contents

contents (continued)

contents (continued)

[AFTER LIFE]

3 REASONS GOD MADE HEAVEN

The Bible is full of teaching on heaven and promises eternal life to all who believe on the Lord Jesus Christ. The Word of God says that every tear will be wiped away, that a mansion is prepared for each one of us, and that we will see our Savior face to face. Here are 3 reasons that God made heaven just for you.

1. **God is a rewarder.** Right now, we serve God by faith, trusting His Word that all He has said is true. Heaven is His reward for our commitment to Him on this earth.

2. **God wants a relationship.** God originally created Adam and Eve in the Garden of Eden and they were sinless, having perfect communion and relationship with Him. God's plan for man all along has been to restore that perfect state of fellowship He once enjoyed with man.

3. **God wants you to reign with Him.** The Bible teaches that we will rule and reign with Christ. (Rev. 20:6.) That means that there are responsibilities and oversight that we will have in heaven. Our minds can't possibly fathom what we will do, but it will be amazing!

3 MISCONCEPTIONS ABOUT HELL

The world and the media don't always paint a very accurate picture of what hell is going to be like for those who reject the forgiveness of Jesus Christ. Here are 3 common misconceptions about eternal damnation as it is described in Scripture. (Matt. 10:28.)

1. **"God sends people to hell."** No, if you end up in hell, it will be because you chose to go there. God is fair and just. He gives every person the opportunity to do the right thing. If we choose to reject His love and commandments, we have made a choice to be separated from Him.

2. **"Hell will be a party place."** How many rock bands have talked about going to hell because that's where "my friends are going to be, and we'll all party together!" Well, your friends may be there, but the

Bible describes it as a place of weeping and gnashing of teeth, not a party.

3. **"Hell can't be any worse than my life right now."** Don't count on it! Sure, life has its ups and downs. But hell only has downs, with no possibility of ever knowing love, joy, happiness, friendship, or even hope ever again. Trust me, things could be worse!

5 THINGS YOU'LL LOVE IN HEAVEN

So, what's to look forward to in heaven? The Bible is actually pretty specific about what heaven will be like, although it will be so much more than our natural minds could possibly comprehend. But here are a few things that are for sure.

1. **No more tears.** (Rev. 21:4.) God will wipe away every tear, and emotional pain will be a thing of the past.

2. **No more death.** (Rev. 21:4.) We will live forever. The aging process will stop, and we will never have to worry about ever losing a loved one.

3. **Worship at the throne.** Can you imagine worshiping Jesus around the throne of God with all the angels of heaven? What an incredible event! (Rev. 5:8-14.)

4. **Meet the saints of old.** What an awesome time we'll have sitting down with saints like Abraham,

Moses, Daniel, Peter, Paul, and others whose stories
and lives we have read about for years!

5. **No more temptation or sin.** Satan will be cast into
the bottomless pit, and we'll have new bodies, free
from the carnal desires of the flesh and human nature.
Everything inside of us will want to please and honor
our God!

4 STEPS TO FINDING FAVOR WITH GOD

Let's be honest. If you can get yourself in favor with the most powerful Person in the universe, you're going to do really well. The great thing is that God has told us clearly in His Word that we can fall into favor with Him. Here are 4 steps to getting there.

1. **Diligently seek after Him.** He promises to reward and bless anyone who wholeheartedly seeks Him. (Heb. 11:6.)

2. **Search out the wisdom of God's Word.** He promises that when we discover His wisdom, we will obtain favor from Him. (Prov. 8:35.)

3. **Develop a lifestyle of praising God without apology.** The churches in the book of Acts were bold to praise God with their voices and found favor with all the people. (Acts 2:47.)

4. **Walk in goodness and integrity towards others.** God promises you favor, but condemns the person who is wicked in his actions. (Prov. 12:2.)

7 BIBLE GUARANTEES FOR ETERNAL LIFE

God's passion is to share an eternal relationship with you. Throughout the Bible, God guarantees that eternal relationship to those who seek Him. In John 5:39, Jesus said that if you look in the Bible for assurance of eternal life, you would find that everything you unearth testifies of Him. God sent Jesus to provide a way for you to be forgiven and enjoy this eternal relationship, both in your life on earth and in the one to come in heaven. Jesus is the only way to eternal life (John 14:6), and God's Word promises that by believing in Him, we will live eternally in heaven. Here are 7 of those biblical promises for eternal life.

1. **God's Word guarantees eternal life to the believer.** First John 2:24-25 says, "Therefore let that abide in you which you heard from the beginning. If what you heard from the beginning abides in you, you also will abide in the Son and in the Father. And this is the promise that He has promised us—eternal life."

God's plan from the very beginning was to share eternity with you. He has promised that if we abide in Him, we will have eternal life.

2. **God's Word guarantees that eternal life is a gift.** In Romans 6:23, the Bible tells us that "the wages of sin is death, but the gift of God is eternal life in Christ Jesus our Lord." The greatest gift that was ever given was Jesus' coming to earth to make a way for a personal relationship with God. That gift makes it possible to escape the wages of sin. You don't have to fear death, because God has offered you eternal life.

3. **God's Word guarantees that the gift of eternal life is given because God loves us.** John 3:16 says, "For God so loved the world that He gave His only begotten Son, that whoever believes in Him should not perish but have everlasting life." A gift is something that is done out of free will and without obligation. God did not have to offer a way for salva-

tion, but He loved the world so much that He made a way for you to know Him.

4. **God's Word guarantees that eternal life is available to everyone.** In Romans 10:13, we find that "whoever calls on the name of the Lord shall be saved." God didn't say that "just people with perfect lives" or "only people who have done enough to earn My love will be saved." His Word says "whosoever." In other words, everyone and anyone who makes the choice will be saved.

5. **God's Word guarantees that we can receive eternal life.** Romans 10:10 say, "For with the heart one believes unto righteousness, and with the mouth confession is made onto salvation." Although there is a part you play in accepting God's gift, it is as simple as believing in what God did, receiving the gift, and confessing Jesus as Lord. God made salvation and eternal life something that anyone can receive.

6. **God's Word guarantees that God has called you to eternal life.** First Timothy 6:12 encourages you to "fight the good fight of faith, lay hold on eternal life, to which you were also called…." You can be encouraged to continue in your relationship with God, because you know that He has called you into His family. It is not accidental; God knows you and desires to have a relationship with you personally.

7. **The Bible guarantees that God created a specific place for you.** In John 14:2, Jesus tells us, "In My Father's house are many mansions; if it were not so, I would have told you. I go to prepare a place for you." Jesus promised that we would have a specific place set aside to enjoy eternity with Him. This is more than just a blanket promise of a vague place called heaven, but it is evidence that God values each of us individually.

[HAPPINESS]

3 THINGS THAT WON'T MAKE YOU HAPPY

Happiness is not an act or an object. Happiness is not an event or goal that you eventually reach. True happiness is not a feeling that you can manufacture or a feeling that happens accidentally. True happiness is a lifestyle. If people are truly happy, it is because of how they live their lives, not because of what they have in their lives. Here are 3 things that seem to make people happy but won't make you truly happy at all.

1. **Fame.** People who are in the spotlight are always smiling. It can even seem as though their lives are perfect. But being famous is no more a guarantee of happiness than being a car is a guarantee of being fast; it is what's under the hood that counts. There are undoubtedly happy famous people, and there is nothing wrong with being famous. More often than not, fame comes from being good at what you have chosen to do with your life. So choose to pursue something that you love, and you will be more likely to be good at

what you do. Who knows, you might even become world famous. But if you pursue fame just to be famous, you will miss out on what you are truly good at. You will miss out on being truly happy. (Ps. 1:2,3.)

2. **Love.** Some of the most powerful emotions in life come from interacting with someone you have romantic feelings for. They can make you feel like the most important person on the planet. It feels like you could do anything and everything; nothing looks wrong or out of place. Then comes the inevitable—they let you down. How could they do that to you? Didn't they love you? Perhaps they did, but the love of another human is never enough to fill a hole in your heart that is meant for a relationship with God. Some people search their whole lives for happiness because they attach it to the way people treat them. People will let you down, but God will always be there for you. Happiness comes from building a foundation in God and placing your relationship on that solid ground. (Matt. 7:24.)

3. **Money.** There is a saying that "money can't make you happy, but the things you can buy with it will." There is an undeniable thrill that comes from being able to buy something that you have always wanted. But that thrill quickly fades, and something else must take the place of the object you just bought. The circle doesn't end for people who place all of their happiness in the stuff they purchase. The objects and the money are not bad at all, but expecting them to make you truly happy will leave you empty. God wants you to have everything that you need, but the things and the money must be kept in perspective. If you honor God first, He will provide all that you need, and happiness too. (Ps. 128:2.)

5 HABITS OF HAPPY PEOPLE

Happy people are not perfect. They are people who have developed habits that help them succeed. Because true happiness is a lifestyle, developing positive life habits will help you overcome obstacles and enjoy happiness too. These are 5 habits of happy people that you can begin to work on in your life.

1. **Happy people work hard.** Hard work can make up for talent. But talent cannot be substituted for hard work. Just because you are good at something doesn't mean that you will automatically succeed. But if you work hard and do your best, you can often develop the skills that you need as you go. Happy people understand that there is no substitute for the fulfillment of working hard.

2. **Happy people plan ahead.** One of the greatest stresses in life is always doing things at the last minute. In order to limit stress, begin to plan ahead.

Whether it is a small area or a large one, planning ahead will help you get all of your details figured out so you can relax and enjoy life.

3. **Happy people budget well (time, energy, and money).** Many people lose their joy because they find themselves in a situation they were not ready for. By budgeting your time, energy, and money, you will ensure that you are prepared for unexpected challenges. Budgeting does not come naturally to most people. It means that you often have to delay gratification. But if you are willing to develop this habit, you will avoid situations that would rob you of your happiness.

4. **Happy people are life-long learners.** Those who are truly happy and fulfilled understand that they do not know everything. There is a mountain of knowledge to be gained in books, the classroom, and other people's experiences. This thought does not need to intimidate you or challenge your ego. It should liberate you as you realize that no one expects you to know

everything. Make the decision to relax and enjoy the process of growing and learning every day.

5. **Happy people never quit.** Some people quit the moment they encounter trouble. But those people who have developed a truly happy lifestyle understand that tough situations don't last, but tough people do. Circumstances do not define happy people. If you develop the habit of perseverance, you will be wiser and more mature after each obstacle you conquer.

4 STEPS TO FINDING FAVOR WITH FRIENDS

Everyone wants to have good friends. In order to have a good friend, you must learn to be one. There are very real reasons why everyone seems to like some people, while others are constantly rejected. Here are 4 practical steps to finding good friends.

1. **Break out of your shell of fear.** Don't wait for people to reach out to you. Be bold to say hello to people and make conversation.

2. **Give friends their space.** Don't monopolize people's time or constantly follow them around. When you begin to smother people with attention, they will naturally want to avoid you.

3. **Be confident in yourself and your abilities.** If you are constantly putting yourself down and wallowing in self-pity, people will tire of you soon.

4. **Have a giving heart without trying to "buy" your friendships.** Be generous and thoughtful without feeling like you have to do things to keep a certain friend. If you have to buy or give someone something all the time, the person is probably not a friend anyway.

3 WORDS HAPPY PEOPLE SAY EVERY DAY

First Peter 3:10 says, "For he who would love life and see good days, let him refrain his tongue from evil and his lips from speaking deceit." God places a great importance on the words that we say. The happiest people in the world aren't always the most bubbly, but they understand the power of their words. By staying positive no matter what the circumstances and always looking to God's promises, happy people win by the words that they say. Here are 3 words that happy people say every day.

1. **"Hello."** Happy people are conscious of others. They think about others before themselves and always try to make people comfortable. A simple greeting can go a long way. Saying "hello" and acknowledging someone's presence can be just the encouragement that person needs. Happy people recognize the importance of a positive demeanor. (Titus 3:15.)

2. **"Thank you."** Truly happy people don't take everyday
    things for granted but stay thankful no matter how big
    or small the gift is. Thankfulness will keep your heart
    pure and help keep you from becoming cynical. (Rom.
    1:21; Ps. 1:1,2.) Happy people are thankful people.

3. **"Fine."** No matter what circumstances happy people
    are going through, when asked how they are doing,
    their response is always representative of the positive
    things going on in their life. They trust God's promises
    to meet any need they face or difficulty they encounter.
    The happiest people in life don't deny the negative;
    they simply focus on the positive. (Heb. 10:23.)

7 BIBLE GUARANTEES FOR HAPPINESS

Remember that true happiness is not an emotion, but it is a lifestyle. Often referred to in the Bible as "joy," true happiness is something God desires for you to have every day of your life. While circumstances and tragedy may seem to take the happiness out of life, God has promised that by walking with Him we can know true happiness in spite of anything that comes our way. There is nothing in life that can bring you happiness like God, and nothing in life can take away the happiness that comes from Him. Here are 7 guarantees from the Bible for true happiness in your life.

1. **God's Word guarantees that if we follow Him, we will have true happiness.** Psalm 144:15 says, "Happy are the people whose God is the Lord." People often look for happiness in the material possessions of this world. But God's Word promises that if we put Him first, we will find fulfillment and live a truly happy life.

2. **God has guaranteed that true happiness is a product of knowing Him.** Galatians 5:22-23 (NIV) says, "But the fruit of the Spirit is love, joy, peace, patience, kindness, goodness, faithfulness, gentleness, self-control." The joy that comes from God's Spirit living in us cannot be manufactured. It is the fruit of a healthy relationship with God.

3. **God's Word guarantees that you will find true happiness when you love people with His love.** Proverbs 14:21 says, "He who despises his neighbor sins; but he who has mercy on the poor, happy is he." It's easy to ask, "What's in this for me?" Loving people who can do something for you is simple. But you have a promise that when you choose to love people regardless of what they can do for you, you will experience a joy that selfish people will never know.

4. **God's Word guarantees that you can be truly happy no matter what problems you face.** James 1:2-4 says, "My brethren, count it all joy when

you fall into various trials, knowing that the testing of your faith produces patience. But let patience have its perfect work, that you may be perfect and complete, lacking nothing." James didn't say to be happy because you come up against problems; he said that because of the joy you have in knowing that God has an answer, even a negative circumstance can have a good outcome. You can actually grow and mature as a Christian by responding to problems with joy, faith, and patience.

5. **The Bible guarantees that your joy will grow as you spend time with God.** Acts 2:28 says, "You have made known to me the ways of life; You will make me full of joy in Your presence." By developing a personal relationship with God and spending time in His presence, you will find joy and fulfillment. God wants to know you personally, and by developing that relationship, you will have happiness that is greater than anything you could ever find on your own.

6. **The Bible guarantees that the true happiness that comes from God will be your strength.** Nehemiah 8:10 says, "...do not sorrow, for the joy of the Lord is your strength." There will be times in life when you feel like you don't know what to do or where to turn, but God has promised that His joy will always be your strength. Even in the midst of tragedy or heartache, if you turn to God, His joy will be more than enough for whatever you face.

7. **The Bible guarantees that your future happiness is secure if you hope in God.** Psalm 146:5 says, "Happy is he who has the God of Jacob for his help, whose hope is in the Lord his God." Knowing that God has always been faithful to those who trust in Him provides hope for your future. No matter what your background or where you come from, if you trust in God, He has promised to be your help and show you the way to succeed.

[FORGIVENESS]

5 REGRETS NO TEEN SHOULD EVER LIVE WITH

The world is full of people who look back with regret on their teenage years. They longingly wish they had done things differently. You have the opportunity right now to assure yourself of no regrets.

Here are 5 regrets you don't want to live with the rest of your life.

1. **Moral regrets.** Don't allow yourself to compromise your purity and be remembered forever with the stains of sexual sin. (Rom. 12:1.)

2. **Ministry regrets.** If the Lord is speaking to you about sharing your faith with a classmate, take the opportunity. It may never come again.

3. **Mentor regrets.** Submit yourself to a good pastor and others you trust to mold you and develop you as a

leader. Now is your greatest time of learning and personal development.

4. **Maximum regrets.** Never leave yourself wondering what could have happened—in school, athletics, church, or any other part of life—if you would have given all you had to give to succeed.

5. **Media regrets.** Don't ever allow yourself to look back at your youth as a time when all you did was watch TV, play video games, and go to movies. Do something productive in your life, along with your entertainment.

2 REASONS YOU MAY NOT FEEL FORGIVEN

When you accept God's forgiveness and confess Jesus as Lord, you are forgiven of all of your sins. (Rom. 10:9,10.) Although you receive a new spirit, your soul (which is made up of your mind, will, and emotions) remains the same. Paul tells us in Romans 12:2 that we must actively renew our minds by spending time in God's Word. Because this is something that we must do ourselves, it does not happen overnight. It takes time for your soul to match up with your spirit. Here are 2 reasons you may not feel forgiven.

1. **Your thoughts.** Once you have confessed your sins, God has promised that He has forgiven you. (1 John 1:9.) Your thoughts, however, will try to tell you other-wise. Because your mind must be continually renewed, you may still have doubts about your forgiveness. You may even think that perhaps God didn't hear your prayer. But no matter what your thoughts tell you, you must believe God's Word over what you think.

2. **Your emotions.** Emotions can be a wonderful thing. They can add excitement as you anticipate an upcoming event and make you happy when something good happens. But, emotions can bring you down in negative circumstances and leave you feeling depressed if something bad happens. As you accept God's forgiveness, your emotions may not confirm that forgiveness. You may still fight feelings of guilt over things you've done in the past. However, the truth is you are forgiven no matter what your emotions tell you. As you trust God and continue to obey His Word, your emotions will begin to line up with the truth of God's Word.

3 WAYS TO KNOW THAT YOU HAVE NOT COMMITTED THE UNPARDONABLE SIN

Perhaps you have heard the term *unpardonable sin* and thought to yourself, *I feel far away from God; how can He forgive me?* or, *How do I know that I haven't sinned too much to be forgiven?* Jesus refers to the sin that isn't forgivable in Matthew 12:31-32. As Jesus was teaching and casting out demons, the religious leaders accused Him of doing this by satanic means. They were so spiritually blind that they gave credit for the work of the Holy Spirit to Satan. It was then Jesus said, "Every sin and blasphemy will be forgiven men, but the blasphemy against the Holy Spirit will not be forgiven." So the unpardonable sin is not simply saying an unkind word about the Holy Spirit; it is rejecting God altogether and being so hard-hearted that you don't know the difference between evil and good. The unpardonable sin is not unforgivable because God doesn't want to forgive it, but because He cannot forgive someone who has rejected Him altogether. Here are 3 ways to know that you have not committed the unpardonable sin.

1. **You have a desire to serve God.** If you want to be obedient to God's Word and serve Him, then God's forgiveness is still available to you. It is those who have hardened their hearts and do not want to receive from God who cannot enjoy His mercy.

2. **You repent and recognize your need for forgiveness.** When you acknowledge your sin and ask God for forgiveness, you become humble and automatically take yourself out of the company of those who are too hard-hearted to turn from sin.

3. **You recognize the difference between good and evil.** The religious leaders in Matthew 12 were so blinded that when Jesus was doing good, they accused Him of working through the power of Satan. When you go to God and say, "God, I recognize that You are holy and that in order to have a relationship with You, my sins have to be forgiven," you are acknowledging that God is good. If you desire for the Holy Spirit to work in your life, you can be at peace knowing that you haven't committed the unpardonable sin.

5 STEPS TO OVERCOMING TOUGH TEMPTATIONS

As you grow in your relationship with God, you will find that there are things that still cause you to be tempted. Even though you are forgiven and walking in relationship with God, these temptations may still be very strong. Here are 5 steps to overcoming even the toughest temptations.

1. **Avoid situations that tempt you.** (Gen. 39:10,11; 2 Tim. 2:22.) One of the best ways to avoid sin is to avoid the situations that you know are a temptation to you. Each person is different, and each person may struggle in different areas after they are born again. But by being humble enough to admit that you are tempted in a certain situation and avoiding that area, you will save yourself heartache down the road.

2. **Keep God's Word in your heart and in your mouth.** (Ps. 119:11.) By keeping yourself full of God's

Word, you automatically reduce your ability to be tempted. (Gal. 5:16.) If you focus on God's promises and His love for you, the payoff for giving in to any temptation seems insignificant.

3. **Choose ahead of time to make the right decisions.** By making the tough choices before you face the temptation, you allow yourself to make decisions in a neutral environment without the heat of emotions. You will always make better decisions if you base them on your integrity. (Prov. 11:3.)

4. **Be careful what you allow to influence you.** (Prov. 4:23.) If you hang around the wrong places or the wrong people for long enough, absolutes can become blurred. By choosing wisely who and what you allow to influence you, you guard yourself from temptation.

5. **Look to God.** It is always better to avoid temptation altogether when possible. But if you do find yourself in a situation where you are tempted to compromise,

remember God has a way out. (1 Cor. 10:13.) If you do the things that you can to avoid temptation, God will be faithful to help you right where you are in your moment of temptation.

7 BIBLE GUARANTEES FOR FORGIVENESS

The foundational element of the Bible is God's plan of redemption for mankind. Throughout the pages of God's Word, you can find His desire for you to be saved. God loved you so much that He did everything to provide forgiveness for you, except make you receive it. That one small part is yours to play. God's forgiveness is available for you today. Here are 7 promises from the Bible that guarantee your forgiveness.

1. **God's Word guarantees that forgiveness is available to everyone regardless of background.** (Rom. 10:13 KJV.) Acts 10:34 says, "Of a truth I perceive that God is no respecter of persons." No matter who you are or where you are from, God's forgiveness is available to you.

2. **God's Word guarantees that if you repent, you will be forgiven.** First John 1:9 says, "If we confess our sins, He is faithful and just to forgive us our sins

and to cleanse us from all unrighteousness."
Forgiveness is obtained by a choice you make to
receive God's gift. Although forgiveness is free, it is
only possible if you humble yourself, admit you were
wrong, and acknowledge your need for God.

3. **God's Word guarantees that you are forgiven
   when you choose to forsake your sin.** Proverbs
   28:13 says, "He who covers his sins will not prosper,
   but he whoever confesses and forsakes them will have
   mercy." God's desire is that you forsake the things that
   cause you to stumble and grow in a relationship with
   Him each day.

4. **God's Word guarantees that Jesus paid the
   price for your forgiveness so that you don't
   have to.** Second Corinthians 5:21 says, "For He
   made Him who knew no sin to be sin for us, that we
   might become the righteousness of God in Him." By
   taking our punishment for us, Jesus made a way for us

to be forgiven. There is no debt left to pay; it's been paid in full

5. **God's Word guarantees that we're forgiven by faith, not by works.** Ephesians 2:8-9 says, "For by grace you have been saved through faith, and that not of yourselves; it is the gift of God, not of works, lest anyone should boast." It's not by your own strength or anything that you've done that you are forgiven. There is nothing you can do to earn your way into heaven. You can't be good enough, work hard enough, or buy your way into heaven. It is simply by the work of Jesus' dying on the cross and rising again that you have been forgiven.

6. **God's Word guarantees that when you are forgiven, God no longer remembers your sin.** Hebrews 10:17 says, "…their sins and their lawless deeds I will remember no more." God's forgiveness is a complete work. The slate is wiped clean. The sin is remembered no more.

7. **The Bible guarantees that God desires to forgive you because of His love for you.**

    Romans 8:32 says, "He who did not spare His own Son, but delivered Him up for us all, how shall He not with Him also freely give us all things?" God's love for you is so great that He gave His own Son to pay the price for your forgiveness. No one forced God to provide a way of forgiveness. He did it because He loves you.

[FRIENDS]

3 KINDS OF PEOPLE WHOSE
FRIENDS ARE FEW

Your friends can be your greatest allies. They can lift you up if you get discouraged and share in your joy and success. Not everyone has friends. Certain kinds of people make a friendship nearly impossible by their lifestyle or attitude. Here are 3 kinds of people whose friends are few.

1. **Negative people.** It's hard to be around people who always see the bad side of things. People who constantly complain about problems are not attractive to spend time with. It is true that there will be things that are not perfect, but focusing on those things causes people to miss out on all of the good things that God has for them and their friends.

2. **Arrogant people.** People who constantly talk about themselves and belittle the accomplishments of others often drive friends away. Friendship is a two-way

street. There must be a mutual interest and respect for any healthy relationship to survive. Arrogant people may act as though they have it all together, but an arrogant attitude is a natural friend repellent that leaves many people lonely.

3. **Cynical people.** A cynical person is someone who is always sarcastic and never appreciates the value of friendship. They often try to be funny at the cost of another person's feelings. The cynic is also someone who takes very little on faith. Without faith and trust, most relationships will fail. Cynical people lose friends by belittling them with their words or showing a lack of faith with their actions.

5 ATTITUDES THAT ARE FRIEND MAGNETS

There are always those people that you are naturally attracted to, those friends that you want to spend all of your free time with. What is it about those people that makes others want to be around them? Here are 5 character traits that make people friend magnets.

1. **Happiness.** Nobody wants to be around a grump. A great attitude is one of the strongest magnets for friends. When you are happy, it's contagious. Always try to stay upbeat, and you will never cease to be in the company of friends.

2. **Encouraging.** Choosing to lift other people up with a kind word or a generous action will naturally draw other people to your side. A word in due season is often just the encouragement someone else needs. (Prov. 15:23.)

3. **Generosity.** Unselfishness has a powerfully attractive force. By choosing to share and think of others before yourself, you show people that you value them.

4. **Objective.** It's nice to be around people who are willing to hear the opinions of others. Let's face it, you're not always right, so pick your battles carefully and be willing to accept someone else's idea if it's better than yours.

5. **Helpfulness.** You're not much of a friend if you're not willing to lend a hand. It works both ways. There will be a time when you need some help, so sow the seeds of friendship now, and you will reap the rewards later.

5 FRIENDS THAT WILL TAKE YOU DOWN

The Bible tells us that those who walk with the wise will be wise, but the companion of fools will be destroyed. (Prov. 13:20.) Here are 5 different kinds of "friends" that can destroy your relationship with the Lord.

1. **The mocker:** the friend who always makes fun of spiritual things.

2. **The doubter:** the friend who believes and talks about the worst; usually the last to acknowledge what God can do.

3. **The compromiser:** the friend who goes to church and talks a good talk but, more often than not, does not back it up with a life that honors God.

4. **The proud:** the friend who thinks he or she is more spiritual than you or anyone else and constantly

displays a critical attitude about everyone else's "lack of commitment."

5. **The gossip:** the friend who always "talks down" other people around you. If a person says negative things to you about his or her other friends, what is the person saying to them about you?

3 MARKS OF A TRUE FRIEND

There is a big difference between an acquaintance and a true friend. People you simply hang out with will come and go, but a true friend is someone who will always be there for you. Recognizing the difference will help you develop relationships that will last. Here are 3 marks of a true friend.

1. **Honesty.** A true friend will tell you the truth no matter what, even if it may initially hurt your feelings. Having someone who will give you an honest answer is priceless. (Prov. 27:6.)

2. **Dependability.** The people who truly value their friendship with you will keep their word. If you cannot count on someone, your friendship will not last.

3. **Respect.** Mutual respect is a large part of a good friendship. If someone is not respected, their opinions and feelings will be discounted and overlooked. Without respect, a friendship will simply not work.

7 BIBLE GUARANTEES FOR FRIENDSHIP

God recognized man's need for relationship when He created a companion for Adam in the Garden of Eden. In Genesis 2:18, God said, "It is not good that man should be alone." We need godly relationships in our lives to strengthen and encourage us. Here are 7 Bible guarantees for friendship.

1. **God's Word guarantees that you will have friends if you show yourself friendly.** Proverbs 18:24 says, "A man who has friends must himself be friendly." The Bible encourages you to take the first step and initiate friendships. You will have quality friends if you make the effort to always be friendly.

2. **God's Word guarantees that godly friends make you stronger.** Proverbs 27:17 says, "As iron sharpens iron, so a man sharpens the countenance of his friend." As you grow in your relationship with God and pursue godly relationships, the friends you choose to surround

yourself with will either move you closer to or further away from your goals. Good friends will sharpen you, because they are moving in the same direction as you.

3. **God's Word guarantees that godly friends will help you realize your potential.** Proverbs 20:5 says, "Counsel in the heart of man is like deep water, but a man of understanding will draw it out." God has a unique purpose for you. Good friendships will help you achieve all that God has planned for your future.

4. **God's Word guarantees that true friends will stick with you no matter what.** Proverbs 17:17 says, "A friend loves at all times, and a brother is born for adversity." Fair weather friends will leave at the first sign of trouble. But true friends do not change their attitude towards you just because negative circumstances arise.

5. **God's Word guarantees that you will become wise if you hang out with wise friends.** Proverbs

13:20 says, "He who walks with wise men will be wise...." Friendships influence almost all of our choices. Surround yourself with wise friends who can help you make wise choices in every area of life.

6. **God's Word guarantees that you can avoid suffering by not hanging out with foolish people.** Proverbs 13:20 says, "...But the companion of fools will be destroyed." This verse warns that if you choose to hang out with foolish friends, you will share the same fate they have. So choose to avoid inevitable heartache by steering clear of those who make bad choices.

7. **God's Word guarantees that you will reap what you sow into your friendships.** Galatians 6:7 says, "...whatever a man sows, that he will also reap." If you spend time developing strong relationships, those relationships can become a great resource. Friendships have to be nurtured in order to thrive. If you take your friends for granted, the relationships will eventually wither and die.

[DIRECTION]

3 KEYS TO EFFECTIVE PLANNING

If you want success, you must plan for it. Someone once asked Wayne Gretzky how he became the best goal scorer in the history of hockey. He replied, "While everyone else is chasing the puck, I go to where the puck is going to be." He planned ahead. Let's take a look at 3 keys to effective planning.

1. **Prayer.** You may not know what the future holds, but God does. God promises that if you will ask Him, He will show you things that you could never figure out on your own. (Jer. 33:3.)

2. **Goal setting.** Write out exactly what it is you are planning for. You will be amazed how this key will unlock your future.

3. **Prioritizing.** You can't keep your priorities if you don't have any. Putting things in order will help you plan and accomplish the most important things first.

5 SOURCES OF RELIABLE COUNSEL

It is important to carefully choose who and what you allow to influence your choices. Some people will have good intentions but lead you astray with their advice. God has placed specific people in your life to speak into your decision-making. There are sources that you should always go to when you are in need of counsel. Here are 5 great sources of reliable counsel.

1. **The Bible.** Psalm 32:8 (NIV) says, "I will instruct you and teach you in the way you should go; I will counsel you and watch over you." The Bible is full of answers to life's most difficult problems. If you are searching for an answer, the Bible is the first place you should look. You should always judge any other advice by what the Bible has to say.

2. **Parents.** God chose your parents to raise you and teach you as you grow and mature. Godly parents

are a blessing, but even if your parents aren't Christians, they can still be a great source of answers to practical questions.

3. **Mentor.** If you don't have a solid parental figure in your life, maybe there is someone you look up to, such as a teacher or coach. Mentors can often provide an objective viewpoint and help you see the whole picture.

4. **Pastor.** God has placed leaders in the church to act as shepherds over believers. As shepherds, it is their job to protect, nurture, and lead you as a Christian. They can be a great source of biblical wisdom and godly counsel.

5. **Holy Spirit.** Jesus gave you the Holy Spirit as your Comforter. He is always with you and will never leave you. John 14:26 says, "He will teach you all things, and bring to your remembrance all things that I said to you."

4 STEPS TO KNOWING GOD'S LEADING

God has promised that He will lead and guide those who diligently follow Him. (Prov. 3:5,6.) There are times when you face a decision and you're not sure which way to go. When there doesn't seem to be a definite right answer, here are 4 questions to ask yourself.

1. **"Do I have peace about it?"** If you are born again, God has promised that the Holy Spirit will lead and guide you into all truth. (John 16:13.) James 3:17 says, "But the wisdom that is from above is first pure, then peaceable…." If it is not a question of right and wrong, the next step is to follow peace.

2. **"Does it line up with God's Word?"** God's Word is constant. (Ps. 119:89.) It is settled. So you will never get a leading that contradicts what God has said in His Word. The Bible is full of wisdom that will help you make good choices.

3. **"Is it a step or a leap?"** Psalm 37:23 says, "The steps of a good man are ordered by the Lord." God leads one step at a time. He will never ask you to do more than you are able. If it feels like a leap, it probably is. Take a step back and reevaluate the situation.

4. **"Is it mutually beneficial?"** God's kingdom operates on a system of exchange. Sowing and reaping, springtime and harvest, and labor and pay are all examples of exchange. God will not lead you to do something that requires you to sacrifice everything without compensation. Long-term, overseas missionaries, for example, have to make sacrifices in order to spread the gospel. But God will not ask you to be a full-time missionary without also giving you ways and means to take care of your family in exchange for being obedient. God know what you need and will be faithful to provide. (Matt. 6:33.) In Matthew 10:10, Jesus said, "A worker is worthy of his food." When God directs you to do something, there will be something beneficial that you bring to the relationship and something good that you take away.

3 KEYS TO DISCOVERING YOUR CAREER

When you are young, your career is more of a dream than a reality. But before you know it, you're well on your way. There are thousands of possibilities for your future profession, but there's something specific that God has planned just for you. It's never too early to begin the process of finding the career that is best suited for you. Here are 3 keys to discovering your career.

1. **Find out what you're good at doing.** Some people are gifted artistically, some musically, some mechanically. Focus on the things that you do well, and begin to develop the skills that correlate. Your future career will likely come from something that you are naturally good at doing.

2. **Try it on for size.** Just because you're good at something doesn't mean you enjoy it. Your career will not last long if you don't enjoy what you are doing.

See if you can do an internship in the career field you are interested in. Maybe you can get a part-time job during the summer.

3. **Narrow down your options.** Take a look at all of the possibilities. Rule out the career choices that you know would not bring you fulfillment and the one you try and dislike. The shorter your list, the more specific training you can seek.

7 BIBLE GUARANTEES FOR DIRECTION

A lack of direction causes many people to wander aimlessly through life. Without direction, it is impossible to know whether or not you are getting anywhere or accomplishing your goals. God has promised throughout His Word that He will guide and direct us. Here are 7 Bible guarantees for direction.

1. **The Bible guarantees that if you trust in God, He will direct your path.** Proverbs 3:5-6 says, "Trust in the Lord with all your heart, and lean not on your own understanding; In all your ways acknowledge Him, and He shall direct your paths." When you limit God's leading to your understanding, you rule out hidden potential. But by acknowledging God in all that you do, you open the door for Him to lead you even if you don't understand it all right away.

2. **The Bible guarantees that God has a plan for your life.** Jeremiah 29:11 says, "For I know the

thoughts that I think toward you, says the Lord, thoughts of peace and not of evil, to give you a future and a hope." This guarantee can strengthen your faith, knowing that God has great things in store for you. God will never forget about you, and no matter where you are, God sees you and has a plan for your success.

3. **The Bible guarantees that God will direct the steps of the righteous man.** Psalm 37:23 says, "The steps of a good man are ordered by the Lord, and He delights in his way." Even though you can't see 50 years into your future, God has guaranteed that He will direct the steps that are in front of you.

4. **The Bible guarantees that the Lord's purpose for you will prevail.** Proverbs 19:21 says, "There are many plans in a man's heart; nevertheless the Lord's counsel—that will stand." No matter what you face or how many people let you down, God's direction and plan for your life will stand strong. Your path to God's best is not dependent on what other people do

or what breaks you catch; it is dependent on your faithfulness to God, and God will never let you down.

5. **The Bible guarantees that the plans of the diligent lead to plenty.** Proverbs 21:5 says, "The plans of the diligent lead surely to plenty, but those of everyone who is hasty, surely to poverty." The Bible promises that if you are diligent and do your part to follow God's direction, the path will always lead to abundance.

6. **The Bible guarantees that if you remain humble, God will guide you.** Psalm 25:9 says, "The humble He guides in justice, and the humble He teaches His way." If you remain humble, you allow God to continually teach and instruct you throughout your life. But if you become proud and unteachable, you limit God's ability to guide you as you grow.

7. **The Bible guarantees that His children will be led by His Spirit.** Romans 8:14 says, "For as many

as are led by the Spirit of God, these are the sons of God." You become a son (or daughter) of God when you are born again. As a child of God, you have a supernatural ability to be led by the Spirit of God. You can stand on His Word, knowing that even in difficult situations, He will be there to lead and guide you.

[MONEY]

3 WARNINGS TO HEED ABOUT MONEY

Perhaps you have heard someone say, "Money is the root of all evil." Hearing this said can make people who don't have money become bitter, and make people who do have money feel bad for having anything at all. It is not written anywhere in the Bible that money is the root of all evil. The Apostle Paul wrote Timothy and warned, "For the love of money is a root of all kinds of evil." While money is neither good nor evil of itself, Paul gave 3 warnings to Timothy that you should heed regarding money. First Timothy 6:10 says, "For the love of money is a root of all kinds of evil, for which some have strayed from the faith in their greediness, and pierced themselves through with many sorrows."

1. **"The love of money is the root of all kinds of evil."** If you allow the love of money to consume you, you become susceptible to all kinds of problems. When you get so focused on making money, the other things in life seem insignificant. Family,

God, community, ethics, and morals all take a back seat to the pursuit of a dollar. The love of money can blind you to reality and cost you the things and people that are actually worth the most.

2. **"Some people, eager for money, have wandered from the faith...."** Placing too high an importance on money will cause you to shift your focus away from the things of God. Compromise starts small, but if you are too focused on money, it can quickly pollute your thinking, and you begin to justify anything and everything by how much money you made. Don't allow the pursuit of money to cost you a relationship with God.

3. **"...and pierced themselves with many sorrows."** Because money is not eternal, pursuing money at the expense of all else will leave you alone and full of sorrow. Guard your future by making wise decisions with money. Keep money in perspective, and you will avoid sorrow and heartache.

5 WAYS TO GET A GREAT JOB

I've held a job since I was 12 years old. I've learned how to
work hard and have never, ever been fired. I've discovered that
if you give your best, you will have the opportunity to eventually do work that you enjoy and get promoted into a really
cool job. Here are 5 ways to land a great job or career.

1. Get out into the workplace and hunt your job down.
   Knock on doors, set up interviews, and learn to sell
   your desire and ability.

2. Be sure you have properly trained and prepared yourself for the job you really want. If it means college,
   find a way to get to college. Read, learn, intern, volun-
   teer, and do whatever it takes to become the best in
   your field.

3. Start out in any company or organization being willing
   to do the small things that other "big shots" aren't

willing to do. It will separate and distinguish you from the pack.

4. Set your sights high. Don't allow your own self-doubt or other people's lack of support to stop you from going after your goals. (Mark 11:24.)

5. Pray and trust God to open up the doors supernaturally. He can, and He will. (Jer. 33:3.)

4 KEYS TO EFFECTIVE BUDGETING AND SAVING

It's really hard to invest money anywhere if you don't have anything left at the end of each month. It is important to develop a financial plan that will ensure that you have money each month to save and invest. Here are 4 keys to doing that.

1. **Know exactly where you are today.** Make out a list of all your monthly income and all your monthly expenses. The goal is to have more income than expenses!

2. **Determine to live below what you earn.** If you are spending all that you earn (or more) make a commitment to cut back expenses anywhere necessary. It may mean cutting out your cable TV or cell phone, but do what it takes!

3. **Live by the 10 percent rule.** Create a budget that allows you to put 10 percent of your income into saving or investment every month.

4. **Don't forget the tithe!** Before you pay a bill or
    make an investment, pay your 10 percent tithes to your
    local church. God will multiply it back abundantly!
    (Mal. 3:10.)

5 OBSTACLES TO PROSPERITY IN YOUR LIFE

God desires for His children to prosper. (Ps. 35:27.) Yet many people struggle their entire lives without ever enjoying God's blessing. If people do not walk in prosperity in the area of their finances, it is because they have allowed at least 1 of these 5 major obstacles to stand in the way of God's best.

1. **Fear.** The greatest obstacle we face is fear. Fear is the most dangerous because it causes faith to become inactive. People who walk in fear financially never make faith choices regarding money and never allow God to work of their behalf.

2. **Doubt.** Many Christians questions whether or not God really wants to bless them. The best way to fight doubt is to speak God's Word over your finances.

3. **Laziness.** God blesses hard work. (Prov. 12:24.) If all you do is sit around and never put action behind your faith, you limit God's ability to work on your behalf.

4. **Arrogance.** First Peter 5:5 says that God resists the proud. God will resist blessing you if you refuse to be humble and are unwilling to be taught.

5. **Greed.** If you are constantly grabbing and holding everything you get with a tight fist, you limit God's ability to bless you in the future.

7 BIBLE GUARANTEES FOR MONEY

God has a great plan for your success. As you follow Him,
He has promised throughout His Word that He will bless and
prosper you. Finding those promises and confessing them
over your life will open the door for God to bless you.
Jeremiah 1:12 says that God is watching over His Word to
perform it. God is waiting for you to believe what He has
said. Here are 7 Bible guarantees that you can stand on for
your finances.

1. **The Bible guarantees that if you acknowledge
   God in your finances, you will prosper.**

   Proverbs 3:9-10 says, "Honor the Lord with your possessions, and with the firstfruits of all your increase,
   so your barns will be filled with plenty and your vats
   overflow with new wine." By putting God first, you
   open the door for His blessing to impact every area of
   your finances.

2. **The Bible guarantees that God honors the tithe.** Malachi 3:10 says, "Bring all the tithes into the storehouse, that there may be food in My house, and try Me now in this, says the Lord of hosts, if I will not open for you the windows of heaven and pour out for you such blessing that there will not be room enough to receive it." When you make the choice to honor God by giving Him the first 10 percent of what you make, He will bless you and meet all your needs.

3. **The Bible guarantees that God will protect your finances.** In Malachi 3:11, God says, "And I will rebuke the devourer for your sakes, so that he will not destroy the fruit of your ground." One of the greatest blessings that you can have when you acknowledge God as your source is His protection over your finances. God will not only bless with more and increase you throughout your life, but He will also safeguard what you already have.

4. **The Bible guarantees that God gives you the power to get wealth.** Deuteronomy 8:18 says, "And you shall remember the Lord your God, for it is He who gives you power to get wealth." God places the ability and the strength to make financial progress in your hand. If you are diligent, God will give you ideas for continued increase.

5. **The Bible guarantees that Jesus broke the curse of poverty.** Second Corinthians 8:9 says, "For you know the grace of our Lord Jesus Christ, that though He was rich, yet for your sakes He became poor, that you through His poverty might become rich." Poverty is not a blessing. God wants you to enjoy His very best. God's plan was never for man to be in lack. Poverty came into the world as part of man's sins. When Jesus died on the cross, He broke the curse of poverty, so that you can enjoy abundance.

6. **The Bible guarantees that God's blessing brings financial prosperity without heartache.**

Proverbs 10:22 says, "The blessing of the Lord makes one rich, and He adds no sorrow with it." When God blesses you, it comes with great joy. The financial prosperity He brings you will never cause you to lose another area of your life. Your family, career, and relationships will only grow because of the blessing He brings you.

7. **The Bible guarantees that God will meet all of your needs.** Philippians 4:19 says, "And my God shall supply all your need according to His riches in glory by Christ Jesus." There is never a need so great that God can't meet it. As you stand in faith for your needs, God will always be faithful to meet them.

PRAYER OF SALVATION

God loves you—no matter who you are, no matter what your past. God loves you so much that He gave His one and only begotten Son for you. The Bible tells us that "...whoever believes in him shall not perish but have eternal life" (John 3:16 NIV). Jesus laid down His life and rose again so that we could spend eternity with Him in heaven and experience His absolute best on earth. If you would like to receive Jesus into your life, say the following prayer out loud and mean it from your heart.

Heavenly Father, I come to You admitting that I am a sinner. Right now, I choose to turn away from sin, and I ask You to cleanse me of all unrighteousness. I believe that Your Son, Jesus, died on the cross to take away my sins. I also believe that He rose again from the dead so that I might be forgiven of my sins and made righteous through faith in Him. I call upon the name of Jesus Christ to be the Savior and Lord of my life. Jesus, I choose to follow You and ask that You fill me with the power of the Holy Spirit. I declare that right now I am a child of God. I am free from sin and full of the righteousness of God. I am saved in Jesus' name. Amen.

If you prayed this prayer to receive Jesus Christ as your Savior for the first time, please contact us on the Web at **www.harrisonhouse.com** to receive a free book.

Or you may write to us at:
Harrison House
P.O. Box 35035
Tulsa, Oklahoma 74153

ABOUT THE AUTHOR

Blaine Bartel founded Thrive
Communications, an organization
dedicated to serving those who
shape the local church. He is also
currently leading a new church launch in a growing area of
north Dallas.

Bartel was the founding youth pastor and one of the key
strategists in the creation of Oneighty®, which has become
one of the most emulated youth ministries in the past decade
reaching 2,500 – 3,000 students weekly under his leadership.
In a tribute to the long term effects and influence of Blaine's
leadership, hundreds of young people that grew up under his
ministry are now serving in full time ministry themselves.

A recognized authority on the topics of youth ministry and
successful parenting, Bartel is a bestselling author with 12
books published in 4 languages, and is the creator of
Thrive—one of the most listened to youth ministry development systems in the country, selling more than 100,000 audio
tapes and CD's worldwide. He is one of the most sought after
speakers in his field; more than one million people from over
40 countries have attended Blaine Bartel's live seminars or
speaking engagements.

His work has been featured in major media including "The Washington Post," CBS' "The Early Show," "The 700 Club," "Seventeen" magazine, as well as newspapers, radio programs, and Internet media worldwide.

Bartel's commitment to creating an enduring legacy that will impact the world is surpassed only by his passion for family as a dedicated father of three children and a loving husband to his wife of more than 20 years, Cathy.

To contact Blaine Bartel,

write:

Blaine Bartel

Serving America's Future

P.O. Box 691923

Tulsa, OK 74169

www.blainebartel.com

*Please include your prayer requests
and comments when you write.*

To contact Oneighty®, write:

Oneighty®

P.O. Box 770

Tulsa, OK 74101

www.Oneighty.com

OTHER BOOKS BY BLAINE BARTEL

every teenager's
Little Black Book
on reaching your dreams

every teenager's
Little Black Book
on how to get along with your parents

every teenager's
Little Black Book
on how to win a friend to Christ

every teenager's
Little Black Book
for athletes

every teenager's
Little Black Book
on cash

every teenager's
Little Black Book
on cool

every teenager's
Little Black Book
on sex and dating

every teenager's
Little Black Book
of hard to find information

Little Black Book
for graduates

Thrive Teen Devotional

The Big Black Book
for parents

Let Me Tell You What
Your Teens Are Telling Me

7 Absolutes to Pray Over Your Kids

Take the Turn for God in Just 5 Minutes a Day

Witty, short, and inspiring devotions for teens from one of America's youth leadership specialists!

Teens can discover a real, action-packed, enthusiastic relationship with God. The thrive.teen.devotional is motivated by a very simple challenge: Give just five minutes a day to God and watch your life turn around.

At the end of eight weeks, the Word of God is going to be more real and alive to teens than ever before as they gain spiritual insights on issues like friendships, self-esteem, and prayer. The good news is that when one's mind is renewed, they experience a radical turnaround in every other area of their life, too.

thrive.teen.devotional
by Blaine Bartel
1-57794-777-0

Available at bookstores everywhere or visit www.harrisonhouse.com

Fast. Easy. Convenient.

For the latest Harrison House product information and author news, look no further than your computer. All the details on our powerful, life-changing products are just a click away. New releases, E-mail subscriptions, Podcasts, testimonies, monthly specials—find it all in one place. Visit harrisonhouse.com today!

harrisonhouse

THE HARRISON HOUSE VISION

Proclaiming the truth and the power
Of the Gospel of Jesus Christ
With excellence;

Challenging Christians to
Live victoriously,
Grow spiritually,
Know God intimately.